27
December

Your birthday book

Your genealogical tree

Great grandfather	Great grandmother	Great grandfather	Great grandmother
born:	born:	born:	born:

Grandmother

born:

Grandfather

born:

Mother

born:

You

born:

From the day you were born you became a part of your family's history. We have all wondered at one time or another about our 'roots'. What kind of people were my family? What did they do? Where they rich or poor? One way to find out about your ancestors is to trace your genealogy or 'family tree'. Genealogy is a fascinating pursuit and looking into your own, or anyone else's, can be like reading a good detective story. The first Greek writings were on ancestry while in the Bible there is a genealogy of the world's population from Adam and Eve onwards.

Today however, scarcely anyone can trace their family back further than the 11th century. But from the 1500s onwards people became enthralled by the subject.

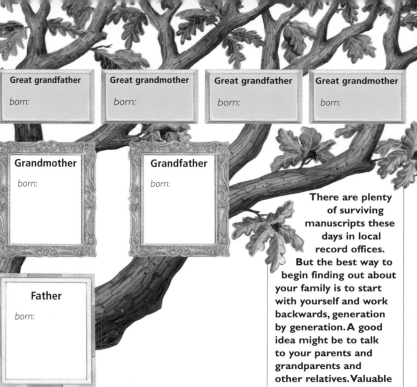

Great grandfather

born:

Great grandmother

born:

Great grandfather

born:

Great grandmother

born:

Grandmother

born:

Grandfather

born:

Father

born:

Brother

born:

or Sister

born:

There are plenty of surviving manuscripts these days in local record offices. But the best way to begin finding out about your family is to start with yourself and work backwards, generation by generation. A good idea might be to talk to your parents and grandparents and other relatives. Valuable information may also be found in old diaries and letters. The further back you go the harder it will become. Who knows what you will find but be prepared: you may stumble upon a few skeletons in your family closet!

The calendars

Needing reliable reference points in time, ancient people began to observe the movements of the Sun, the Moon and the stars in order to establish cycles. Thus shepherds and navigators soon realised that they could use the sky as a clock and a calendar. Thanks to the Sun's regular progress around the Earth, men had a measure for time from very early on: daytime. Then by observing the return of the Sun to the same place on the Earth's horizon, they found another measure: the year, which corresponds with about 12 rotations of the Moon in the sky. The year was therefore divided up into 12 months, enough to lead to the introduction of a calendar which has ruled our lives for more than 4,000 years.

The Sun and the Moon follow different rhythms. Some people base their calendar on the Moon's

cycle and others on the Sun's. Whichever calendar we follow, its function is to give us the feeling that time is passing… and of course, no calendar, no birthday either…

The Earth turns on its axis from east to west and travels around the Sun.

The Earth is one of the nine planets which revolve around a star, the Sun, and which together make up our solar system. The Sun is a burning ball of hot gases which is 100 times bigger than the Earth. It is just one star among the hundreds of millions which make up our galaxy, but it is the closest to the Earth.

The Earth takes 24 hours to turn on its axis: one day. The Moon, going through its phases (see opp. page) takes 29½ days to travel around the Earth: one lunar month. As for the Earth, it takes 365 days and

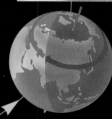

6 hours to travel around the Sun: one year. The solar year is split into 12 months and 11 days. The remaining days are added to the end of certain months: these have 31 days instead of 30.

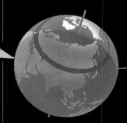

The two hemispheres have opposite seasons.

The Zodiac

The constellations of the Zodiac also gave people the means to combine their dreams with their observations and invent magical stories. Very soon astrologers were using the position of the planets in the Zodiac to predict the future. The planets and stars had a significance and secret meaning which influenced our moods, our character and our life. Astrology, the 'science of the stars', was Mankind's first attempt to understand his world.

From their observations of the sky, ancient people noticed that groups of stars, now called constellations, made shapes which they soon named. At first, these shapes helped to identify specific stars, allowing people to navigate the globe long before the invention of the compass. Then they realised that, seen from the Earth, the Sun, the Moon and the other planets traced a large circle in the sky which led them steadily back through the same constellations. As most of these were named after animals, this circle was called the Zodiac, a Greek word meaning 'circle of animals'. The Sun remains for one month in each constellation: where it was on your birthday determines your 'zodiacal sign'.

The Zodiac

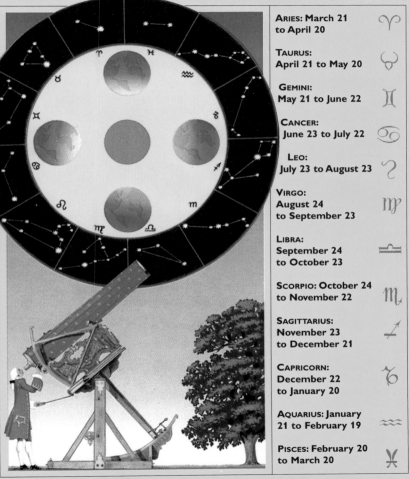

ARIES: March 21 to April 20 ♈

TAURUS: April 21 to May 20 ♉

GEMINI: May 21 to June 22 ♊

CANCER: June 23 to July 22 ♋

LEO: July 23 to August 23 ♌

VIRGO: August 24 to September 23 ♍

LIBRA: September 24 to October 23 ♎

SCORPIO: October 24 to November 22 ♏

SAGITTARIUS: November 23 to December 21 ♐

CAPRICORN: December 22 to January 20 ♑

AQUARIUS: January 21 to February 19 ♒

PISCES: February 20 to March 20 ♓

9

The planets and their influence

Each of the planets has its own properties, just like the signs of the Zodiac on which they are thought to have a ruling influence. The planet Mars governs Aries, Pluto governs Scorpio; Venus governs Taurus and Libra; Saturn governs Capricorn, Mercury governs Virgo and Gemini; Jupiter governs Sagittarius; Neptune governs Pisces and Uranus governs Aquarius. The Sun, centre of our solar system and worshipped for thousands of years under many names, governs Leo – often called the 'Royal Sign' – and finally the Moon which governs the sign of Cancer.

Astrologers have always believed that the Sun, the Moon and the other planets of our solar sytem have a special relationship with one or more signs of the Zodiac, which adds to the subtle complexity of astrology. Not only do they think we are influenced by our zodiacal sign, but the relative positions of all the planets on the exact day and time of our birth is also thought to influence the kind of person we will grow up to be.

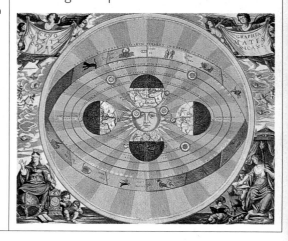

We know that the Moon causes tides in the oceans, and that earthquakes have been attributed to its gravitational force. But from earliest times it was also thought to influence our moods: some people are indeed deeply affected by it – the word 'lunatic' comes from the belief that madness was caused by the phases of the Moon. Many myths grew up around it: in India it was believed that the Moon was the Sun's unfaithful bride, cut in two and only occasionally allowed to shine in her full beauty.

Our solar system, with the nine heavenly spheres.

Your star sign – Capricorn

Ambitious, hard-working and realistic, Capricorns make faithful friends – and relentless enemies. Their motto is 'I master'. They sacrifice their own immediate gratification for long-term achievements and more enduring goals. Their frugal, persevering and industrious approach often leads to great

Capricorns are the truest servants of humanity in the Zodiac. Patient and persistent, they work for the highest ideals but, like the mountain goat, they climb the greatest heights in solitude.

December 22 – January 20

Saturn is Capricorn's ruling planet. Said to be dark, and fateful, Saturn also stands for structure, order and responsibility. Each sign is divided into three 'decans' or periods of ten days. These too have their own characteristics. December 22–January 1 is Capricorn's first decan, January 2–11 is the second and January 12–20 is the third. Common to all three, however, is Capricorn's dependable nature and capacity for great understanding.

success and material wealth. However, Capricorns are prone to periods of doom and gloom and should seek out cheerful company when they feel depression coming on. Each zodiacal sign is also associated with colours, plants, animals and so on that are thought to be beneficial. Capricorns favour dark, rich colours such as purple, black and brown; their gemstone is the tourmaline; their tree is the hawthorn; their animals are the bear, the goat, and the turtle. Saturday is Capricorn's special day.

The stars of your decan

of Jesus, or Jesuit Order. Blazing a trail is **Kit Carson** (Dec. 24, 1809), frontiersman, trapper, soldier, Indian agent and one of America's greatest folk heroes. Two

The constellation Sagitta, traditionally symbolising a heavenly arrow speeding towards its target, is associated with the first decan of Capricorn. Possessing keen minds with the ability for abstract thought, people born in this decan are the ambitious realists.

Bringing a holy light to your decan is **Saint Ignatius de Loyola** (Dec. 24, 1491, middle), founder of the Society

political giants stand out: US President **Woodrow Wilson** (Dec. 28, 1856, left), who sowed the seeds of the League of Nations, and China's Chairman **Mao Zedong** (Dec. 26, 1893 above right), whose Cultural Revolution changed beyond recognition the lives of millions. Further back in time there are

England's **King John** (Dec. 24, 1167 below) whose despotic inclinations led to civil war, and the **Marquise de Pompadour** (Dec. 29, 1721, far right), the favourite of Louis XV and the power behind the French throne. The piled-on-top hairstyle she created still bears her name. Other ambitious realists of your decan include **Lorenzo de' Medici** (Jan. 1,

14

1449), whose power and wealth allowed his passion for art to prosper, while **Louis Pasteur** (Dec. 27, 1822) lent his passion for science to the well-being of mankind. Upping the glamour stakes are Danish supermodel **Helena Christiensen** (Dec. 25, 1968) and German screen siren **Marlene Dietrich** (Dec. 27, 1904), whose on-screen sophistication and sensuality were matched off-screen by numerous night-club appearances during which she had audiences eating out of her hands. Sophistication is also the key word for ultra-cool Scottish diva **Annie Lennox** (Dec. 25, 1954), who has brought sweet dreams to fans world-wide. A quartet of male stars likewise set hearts a-flutter: **Sir Anthony Hopkins** (Dec. 31, 1937), who has played psychopaths and reticent butlers with equal accomplishment; the larger-than-life French Cyrano **Gérard Depardieu** (Dec. 27, 1948); the black star whom America takes seriously, **Denzel Washington** (Dec. 28, 1954); and king of the tough guys, **Humphrey Bogart** (Dec. 25, 1899), whose trademark stiff upper lip was actually caused by an accident involving a splinter.

Finally, two motor men, **Louis Chevrolet** (Dec. 25, 1878) and **Charles Goodyear** (Dec. 29, 1800); two artists, **Maurice Utrillo** (Dec. 25, 1883) and **Henri Matisse** (Dec. 31, 1869); a bright new star on the golf circuit, **Tiger Woods**, (Dec. 30, 1976), and **Helena Rubinstein** (Dec. 25, 1870), founder of the cosmetics empire.

Star of the day

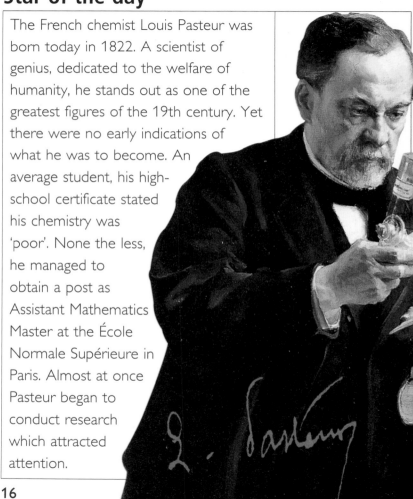

The French chemist Louis Pasteur was born today in 1822. A scientist of genius, dedicated to the welfare of humanity, he stands out as one of the greatest figures of the 19th century. Yet there were no early indications of what he was to become. An average student, his high-school certificate stated his chemistry was 'poor'. None the less, he managed to obtain a post as Assistant Mathematics Master at the École Normale Supérieure in Paris. Almost at once Pasteur began to conduct research which attracted attention.

His work on fermentations laid the foundation for all modern bacteriology, and he also developed the process now known as 'pasteurisation' for sterilising substances and fluids, most commonly milk. He was rewarded with the position of Director of Scientific Studies, but his funding was so low it hardly paid for a laboratory, let alone his research costs. An attack of paralysis, which permanently affected his walk, also added to his difficulties.

However, his financial situation changed when in 1885 he developed an anti-rabies vaccine and used it to save the life of nine-year-old Joseph Meister who had been bitten by a rabid dog. Within days he found himself besieged by crowds of people who had suffered from dog bites. Up until then, rabies was an incurable disease and anyone suffering from it had little chance.

A wave of enthusiasm followed, which led to the foundation of the Pasteur Institute three years later. There, Pasteur was able to continue with his research. He died in 1895, but through the Institute his work continued. Perhaps its most notable success was the discovery of an anti-tetanus vaccine in 1926 – tetanus was a common cause of death at the time, before a treatment was found.

Today in the world

In the city of Tehran the Government decreed today in 1934 that Persia, once one of the most powerful empires in the world, would from this day forward be known as **Iran**. The new country was to be ruled over by Reza Khan (below), a former Cossack who in 1925 had proclaimed himself King.

For the first time in the history of aviation an aircraft was successfully **hijacked** today in 1961 when an international flight was held up by Cuban rebels and forced to land in Havana, Cuba.

J. M. Barrie's fairy-tale adventure *Peter Pan* was first performed at the Duke of York's Theatre in London today in 1904. The play, subtitled *The Boy Who Wouldn't Grow Up*, was an instant success and remained at the Duke of York's for the next ten years. No expense was spared in the production and elaborate effects included birds swooping down to carry off actors, a crocodile eating a wooden boat and Peter sailing off in a huge bird's nest. As well as new effects, the play also gave to the world a new name for girls – Wendy.

Astronauts in the spaceship **Apollo 8** returned to Earth today after making no less than ten orbits of the Moon. The first manned mission to the Moon, the astronauts did not land but had nevertheless proved that they could get there. The following year, on July 21, astronaut Neil Armstrong would go one better when he not only got to the Moon but stepped on to it as well.

Gustave Eiffel, designer of the Parisian landmark which bears his name, died today in 1923. Proposals to build a great tower as part of the Universal Exhibition of 1889 had attracted various grandiose designs. Eiffel – a veteran engineer, who had designed the metal framework of the Statue of Liberty – made his submission in 1885 which was selected as a bold statement of France's industrial power. When it was completed in 1889 it was, at 300m (almost 1,000 ft), the tallest man-made structure in the world. Ironically, Eiffel was himself not a big man at all, and stood only 1.64m or 5ft 4½.

Leon Trotsky, one of the leading lights of the 1917 Russian Revolution, was expelled from the Communist Party by his rival Joseph Stalin today in 1927, and later banished from Russia. In the end Stalin had

him murdered.

And finally, **King Charles II** passed an act 'for erecting and establishing a Post Office' today in 1660. For centuries the wealthy had paid messengers to carry important news (the most famous example is the Greek soldier who in 490BC ran some 24 miles to announce that the Battle of Marathon had been won), but it was a long time before the service was in any way formalised.

Event of the day

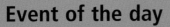

Luckily, Darwin's mind suitably impressed the cautious Fitzroy even if his nose was less promising. On December 27, 1831 Darwin set off from Plymouth aboard **HMS Beagle**.

Our understanding of the world might be very different today if Captain Robert Fitzroy had not changed his mind about Charles Darwin's nose. The captain had written to Cambridge University offering part of his cabin aboard HMS *Beagle* to any man who would go with him as a naturalist on a five-year voyage. Darwin applied, but the captain met him and doubted whether, with a nose like that, the young man would have the energy for such an expedition.

Darwin sets sail

The 23-year-old naturalist could not possibly have predicted the impact that this trip across the Atlantic would have on his career. It was during this voyage that he began to develop his revolutionary theory of evolution: that all species evolve and change as a result of genetic mutations and environmental pressures. These ideas were never more clearly illustrated than on the Galapagos Islands. Here one species of finch had arrived on the islands and, finding no birds to compete with, it had diversified into many sub-species to make the most of the different habitats and foods available. It was as a result of such discoveries that in 1859 Darwin published his deeply controversial book *The Origin of*

Species which claimed, among other things, that the world could not possibly have been created in seven days and that man, far from having been created in the image of God, had descended from apes. The impact of the book was massive, causing much controversy between the religious authorities and the scientific world.

Darwin's theory is now generally accepted as offering the best account of the way different species behave and develop. Small wonder, then, that in his autobiography he called the voyage 'the most important event in my life'.

Inventions of the month

Every month, if not every day, has its own share of inventions, great or otherwise, which have influenced our everyday lives. December is no exception.

The **screw**, the most basic fastening of the

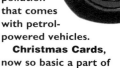

engineer and the do-it-yourself enthusiast, was patented on December 7, 1784 by David Wilkinson, of Rhode Island.

The first wooden **golf tee** – earlier golfers had had to make do with a small pile of earth – was patented by George F. Brant from Boston on December 12, 1899.

On December 5, 1893 the first **electric car** was launched in Toronto, Canada. For a while electric cars rivalled their petrol-driven cousins, but petrol soon won out – although electricity, if only

the batteries could be made powerful and long-lasting enough – is seen once more as a way of combating the pollution that comes with petrol-powered vehicles.

Christmas Cards, now so basic a part of the annual festivities,

were created by Henry Cole on December 9, 1843. Usually, like everyone else, he sent polite notes, but this year he had left it too late. Instead he hired an artist, had a card designed, and sent it along to the printer. His card showed his family sitting round the table, their glasses raised to the absent guest.

December

Digital watches were announced in December 1967 by Switzerland's Horological Electronic Centre on behalf of the 31 Swiss watch manufacturers who had worked on the idea for five years.

King Camp Gillette patented the world's first **safety razor** on December 2, 1901. The original idea behind the razor was not so much the safety factor as the thought that its blades would be disposable. The obvious profit potential of a product that is bought, used, disposed of, and then bought again, was not lost on Gillette. Finally, the upright

A Merry Christmas

vacuum cleaner was first advertised on December 5, 1908 in the *Saturday Evening Post*. The invention of a janitor from Ohio named J. Murray Spangler, it was soon picked up by one W. H. Hoover, who paid only $70 for the idea and went on to make his fortune.

Activated by a battery, the quartz crystal oscillator vibrated 8,192 times a second. The watches sold at huge prices starting at $500.

The seasons

The tropical zone is found between the Tropics of Cancer and Capricorn. Its main characteristics are its almost continuous sunny weather, and the fact that the days are much the same length whatever the season.

In winter, nature sleeps and everything is still. The days are cold and short, the ground hard and food scarce. Some mammals hibernate and in icy northern countries most birds migrate.

But as the English poet Shelley reminds us in his 'Ode to the West Wind': 'If Winter comes, can Spring be far behind?'

24

A regular visitor to North American bird tables is the red cardinal, easily recognised by its tuft and bright plumage. The sparrow, found all over Europe and Asia, is a gallant little bird. In Japan it forms huge and fearless flocks which have no hesitation in venturing into populated areas. The blackbird is a fine songster, but it will feed on fruit and seeds when the ground is too hard to dig for worms. The most cherished of British birds, the robin redbreast, becomes bold in winter and ventures right up to sit on window-sills.

Festivals of the month

A special star rose over Bethlehem on December 25 nearly 2,000 years ago to mark the birth of Jesus Christ. His birthday, **Christmas Day**, is a time of the greatest rejoicing for Christians everywhere, accompanied by rich feasts, serious shopping and presents brought by Santa Claus (left). In stark contrast, for Muslims the month-long sacred fast of **Ramadan** begins in December, when they abstain from food and drink from sunrise till sunset and continue to pray towards Mecca (right). The winter solstice (Dec. 21) was eagerly welcomed in the former festival of **Yule** when the shivering Western nations celebrated the moment when days began to lengthen. In South India it is sunny and mild at this time of year but **Pongal** (Dec.–Jan.) is another festival linked to the solstice. The previous month is considered unlucky and its end is greeted with great happiness by Hindus. Married women cook a dish of rice, milk and jaggery (a kind of unrefined palm sugar) and when it boils they cry out 'Pongal!' ('It's boiling!'), and distribute portions to the temple, the sacred cows and their families. In Mexico the **Virgin of Guadalupe** is honoured by worshippers dragging themselves on their knees to her shrine on Tepeyac Hill in Mexico City, and Oaxaca hosts the **Festival of Radishes** with artisans displaying elaborately carved radishes, including entire Nativity scenes. Saint Nicholas has his day on December 6, and Belgian and Dutch children leave shoes out with a carrot and sugar the night before as a reward for his horse. Jewish homes celebrate the survival of their

December

faith with **Hanukkah**
(between Nov. 25 and
Dec. 26), when a
candle is lit on each
of the seven branches
of the menorah
(candelabrum
symbolic of
Judaism), in
remembrance of
the miracle when
a one-day jar of
oil lit the temple

lamp for eight days.
New Year's Eve (Dec.
31) signals unrestrained
merriment around the
world. In Japan, the
festival of **Omisoka**
is a time to settle
accounts, while in
Ashikaga celebrants
climb to the Saishoji
temple for a
Cursing Festival.
They curse

everything and so rid
themselves of anger.
Finally, in Sweden, **St
Lucy's Day** (Dec. 13) is
a time when the oldest
girl of the family, brings
cakes to the adults,
while her sisters follow
with candles. Processions
also take place to thank
St Lucy for bringing
light and hope at the
darkest time of the year.

27

The internationally famous sleuth, Sherlock Holmes, resident of 22b Baker Street in London, was 'born' on December 1 in 1887 when Arthur Conan Doyle published his first story featuring the great detective: 'A Study in Scarlet'.

BAKER STREET W1

CITY OF WESTMINSTER

Sherlock Holmes

In this Number Solves
The Mystery of

The
Norwood Builder

The story was published in *Beetons's Christmas Annual* and for it Doyle received £25. Doyle had only recently qualified as a doctor and had set up in practice at Southsea, when, as one story goes, he received an unexpected visit from the police after a young patient's death which inspired him to start writing detective fiction. Immediately he hit upon exactly the right formula. The lean, hawk-eyed Holmes solved crimes by sticking to the facts yet was able to deduce from even the smallest details, as if by magic, the most remarkable conclusions.

The first Sherlock Holmes mystery

The famous detective is often said to be based on one of Doyle's lecturers at Edinburgh University, Dr Joseph Bell, but Conan Doyle's son, Adrian, had no doubt that his father was the real Sherlock Holmes: 'In power of deductive observation,' he recalled, 'I have never known his equal.' Doyle's mysteries were serialised in the *Strand Magazine* and stories such as 'The Hound of the Baskervilles' (1902) made his hero one of the world's most loved fictional characters. In all, Doyle wrote 63 stories involving Holmes and his sidekick Watson. In 1894 he tried to kill his hero off but such was the outcry that he had to bring him back to life in 1903. Despite his creation's devotion to cold, hard logic, Doyle was something of a fantasist and in 1920, ten years before his death, went so far as to write an article which claimed to prove once and for all the existence of fairies.

Last words...

'I think, therefore I am,' wrote the French philosopher René Descartes. Here are some of the thoughts people have had on December 27.

1834

My bed fellows are cramp and cough – we three all in one bed. (last words)
Charles Lamb (1775–1834) *English writer*

1857

The commonest and cheapest sounds, as the barking of a dog, produce the same effect on fresh and healthy ears that the rarest music does. It depends on your appetite for sound. Just as a crust is sweeter to a healthy appetite than confectionery to a pampered or diseased one. It is better that these cheap sounds be music to us than that we have the rarest ears for music in any other sense.
Henry David Thoreau (1817–64) *American essayist, poet and naturalist*

1870

Across the fields to the Draycot water. A large fire of logs burning within an enclosure of wattled hurdles. Harriet Awdry skated beautifully and jumped over a half-sunken punt. Arthur Law skating jumped over a chair on its legs.
Francis Kilvert (1840–79) *English country cleric and diarist*

1964

If you resolve to give up smoking, drinking and loving, you don't actually live longer; it just seems longer.
Clement Freud (1924–) *British broadcaster*